Chasing the Flying Snail

Anthony Burges

Colourpoint Books

Chasing the Flying Snail

To Richard S Joby of Norwich for introducing me to the delights of the Irish railways more than half a century ago.

6 5 4 3 2 1

Designed by Colourpoint Books, Newtownards
Printed by: ColourBooks Ltd

ISBN 1 904242 51 0

Colourpoint Books
Colourpoint House
Jubilee Business Park
21 Jubilee Road
Newtownards
County Down
Northern Ireland
BT23 4YH
Tel: 028 9182 0505
Fax: 028 9182 1900
E-mail: info@colourpoint.co.uk
Web-site: www.colourpoint.co.uk

Although English by birth Tony Burges has Irish family connections; his grandfather was from Tralee. He was very active as photographer of UK & Irish branch line railways in the period 1951–1959. He studied transportation at graduate school at Northwestern University, Chicago and photographed railways extensively in the United States. He later worked for the Canadian government as Transport Policy Advisor, Dept of Finance and Director General, Grain Transportation and Handling. He is now semi-retired and devoting time to writing railway books.

Unless otherwise credited all photographs are by the author or taken from the author's collection.

Front cover: A long lost boat train, the 6.15am Saturdays only Rosslare Harbour–Cork via Dungarvan buffet car train, pauses at Mallow on 4 April 1953 for passengers connecting to the Killarney and Tralee line. A remarkably clean class D11 4-4-0 No 302, a Coey design of 1900, provides the power for this 135 mile, 4 hours 15 minute cross country journey.

Rear cover: Metropolitan-Vickers/Crossley A41 passes Amiens Street on 11 September 1957 with a Dublin Westland Row to Galway train composed of the usual mix of rolling stock but typifying a period of major and continuing change on CIÉ.

Foreword

by Dr DB McNeill

One of the most interesting decades in Irish railway history was the 1950s, for it was an age of great transition. When the decade opened steam was providing motive power, rolling stock consisted of vintage carriages and wagons and the majority of branch lines were still open. Ten years later diesel power had displaced steam, new rolling stock had been obtained for a few of the main line services and most of the branch lines had been closed down. The spirit of the decade has been faithfully recorded by the excellent photographs and evocative text of Mr Burges, who travelled extensively in Ireland in the 1950s, in the first of this new series from Colourpoint Books.

Dr DB McNeill
Newtownards, Co Down
September 2005

Introduction

Chasing the Flying Snail

In 1953, a process had already begun which would totally transform the rail system operated by Córas Iompair Éireann (CIÉ); it would have been difficult then to anticipate the magnitude of the changes that subsequently transformed a sprawling but inadequate rail network into the modern, if lean and mean, system that reflects the successful business-oriented nation that has superceded the Ireland of the 1950s. What remains today may be likened to a tree that has been rigorously pruned and is now showing signs of regeneration.

But fifty years ago the picture was very different. To put it bluntly, much of CIÉ had the appearance and atmosphere of an operating museum. That, of course, was part of the undoubted charm which attracted many railway enthusiasts with a keen sense of the past; I count myself among that fraternity.

There was, however, a more serious side to the situation that was to have a profound impact on the future evolution of the system. CIÉ could then be compared to a patient on the critical list; it was clearly facing a crisis. It was obvious that years of deferred maintenance, a fleet of life-expired steam power and rolling stock, and escalating operating losses had resulted in a rail network that required huge investment if it was to serve a useful purpose and offer value to the government and Irish people. The inevitability of change was even more obvious than in the UK. It was ironic that the railway iconography of the time was strangely appropriate in that the CIÉ logo bore a vague resemblance to a flying snail!

In an age when low cost airlines were unknown and car ownership was not commonplace, the ferries and their rail connections were still a dominant means of travel to and from the United Kingdom. Whether one arrived from Holyhead or Fishguard, the rail access to both Dun

Weekday travel times on selected main lines from Dublin summer 1951

Route			Distance (Miles)	Daily Trains	Fastest Time & Av. Speed	Slowest Time & Av. Speed
Dublin AS	–	Cork	172.25	1*	3hr 45 (45.93 mph)	
Dublin K	–	Cork	165.50	5	4hr 05 (40.53 mph)	6hr 30 (25.46 mph)
Dublin K	–	Waterford	110.80 (via Portlaoise)	2	3hr 30 (31.66mph)	
Dublin HS	–	Rosslare Hbr	101.00	2	4hr 00 (25.25 mph)	5hr 05 (19.87 mph)
Dublin WR	–	Rosslare Hbr	102.50	1	4hr 40 (21.96 mph)	
Dublin WR	–	Galway	127.75 (via Mullingar)	4	4hr 00 (31.94 mph)	4hr 35 (27.87 mph)
Dublin WR	–	Westport	162.25 (via Mullingar)	3	6hr 00 (27.04 mph)	6hr 20 (25.62 mph)
Dublin WR	–	Sligo	135.25	3	4hr 50 (27.98 mph)	4hr 55 (27.51 mph)

* 'Enterprise' express

Laoghaire and Rosslare created a lasting impression and an almost surreal sense of time travel. The boat train from Dun Laoghaire to Dublin Westland Row (now Pearse) offered the delights of travel in six wheel carriages hauled by venerable tank engines. Rosslare was even more extraordinary in that the pier had no road access and motorists were obliged to use a rail shuttle service to the mainland, hauled by a somewhat grimy J15 0-6-0 with passengers riding in ancient compartment coaches and cars travelling on flat wagons, a process that could be quite time consuming.

At that time, Ireland had a predominantly rural economy in which the railway was a valued and important source of employment as much as a means of transport. Almost every community had relatively easy access to the railway. The proliferation of quiet, but fully staffed, country stations with carefully tended gardens plus a network of somnolent branch lines had been built for another era in which the population was much larger and transport alternatives were limited. Parts of the system existed in a state of intermittent hibernation that was broken only by a monthly cattle train. Notwithstanding the geographic extent of the network, travel was impeded by the general infrequency and slow speed of the services provided.

But this was a period in which there was truly 'time enough'. This was particularly evident when the traveller was obliged to resort to the use of mail trains which had a nasty habit of reaching their destinations at a time when all self-respecting accommodation for visitors had locked its doors for the night. A tabulation of main line services based on the public timetable illustrates the scheduled performance prior to the introduction of diesel and diesel electric power as a replacement for steam. Timekeeping was poor due to motive power, coal quality, track maintenance standards and signalling conditions so the times shown opposite were not always attained.

On my first visit I remember being fascinated by the impressive terminal stations in Dublin which had changed little since the nineteenth century. Kingsbridge (later Heuston) was particularly grand as befitted the gateway for the main line to Cork, while the extensive trainshed at Westland Row (later Pearse) offered welcome shelter at a time when its always seemed to be raining. Harcourt Street seemed to be a wry joke perpetrated on Dubliners in 1859, as behind its extensive classical façade, there lurked a very modest one platform train shed. A visit to Broadstone revealed more restrained architectural classicism. Although passenger trains had vacated the premises, the array of steam veterans at the shed provided solace. Dublin is fortunate to have retained all of these fine buildings rather than enduring their replacement by mid-twentieth century brutalist structures as occurred all too often elsewhere.

A short bus trip from the city to Inchicore works and shed was a perfect introduction to the array of steam locomotives inherited from the predecessor companies that formed the Great Southern Railway prior to the formation of CIÉ in 1944. What a delight Inchicore was for the photographer with its variety of power ranging from discarded and life-expired locomotives from both broad and narrow gauge; the hush-hush initial turf burning experiment of OVS Bulleid which was tucked away in an obscure corner, and resembled some outrageous vacuum cleaner on wheels; to gleaming, recently-delivered AEC railcars which heralded the onset of modernisation. Another treat was to be found in the form of a shabby, but more or less complete, Drumm battery railcar unit. At Inchicore, locomotives, like old soldiers, did not die, they just faded away.

Inchicore brought a hint of the delights to come, and there was a real sense of adventure when departing from Westland Row on the morning train for Sligo. On the footplate, I soon discovered that the coal available was quite deplorable in quality and consisted partly of coal/cement briquettes which had a habit of disintegrating on hitting the firebars thereby impeding efforts to maintain boiler pressure whilst blanketing the countryside with clouds of pungent, black smoke. Stops at major stations were generous as it was generally understood that passengers would avail themselves of the liquid refreshment facilities available at stops such as Mullingar and Longford. The journey along the former Midland Great Western brought some abiding impressions of impressive semaphore signals and stern, but monumentally solid, station buildings that had obviously been designed to survive the next millennium.

A subsequent trip from Sligo gave an insight into the bucolic delights of the former Waterford, Limerick and Western route to Claremorris and Athenry. The journey on the once-daily train on this western backwater, where stops were made at all stations to exchange the staff and a bit of gossip, was seldom impeded by the appearance of passengers. Our stately 4-4-0 made unhurried progress, scarcely disturbing the peace and quiet that prevailed in the small towns. In 1968 I explored Charlestown which at the time was in the midst of rapid decline. By 2000, the reversal in Irish fortunes has brought new prosperity and the beginnings of a lobbying campaign for the restoration of the rail link from Sligo to Limerick.

Arrival at the junction of Athenry brought the relative bustle of the main line to Galway which seemed to be a stronghold of the Woolwich-built Moguls and offered levels of speed and patronage that were more encouraging. Two delightful vignettes that are engraved in my memory are the Galway–Tuam local noted at Athenry and a glimpse of the Loughrea branch train at Attymon Junction. To the east, and located in the centre of Ireland, Athlone was a railway hub at which four routes met. Since the 1950s, the town has witnessed major changes following the rerouting of trains from the Galway and Westport lines to Dublin away from the old Midland Great Western Railway (MGWR) route via Moate and Mullingar. As a consequence of the old line being mothballed on an indefinite basis, the former Great Southern & Western Railway (GSWR) route from Athlone to Tullamore and Portarlington was transformed from a sleepy backwater across the bogs of Counties Westmeath and Offaly. It had long been an established domain of J15 0-6-0s handling twice-daily passenger trains on weekdays only. Its reincarnation as the new main line from Athlone to Dublin also resulted in the resurrection of the long-closed GSWR station in Athlone and the closure of its former MGWR counterpart on the west bank of the River Shannon. Now the old main line between Athlone and Mullingar is silent and in limbo, awaiting an uncertain fate, although reopening remains a distant prospect. Such changes illustrate the degree of unpredictability and innovation that is a welcome feature of Irish railway development in the twenty first century.

Continuing on what was a circuitous and erratic journey around Ireland in 1953 I made notable excursion along one of the more forgotten sections of CIÉ. This was on the weekdays-only all-stations passenger train from Limerick to Tralee via Newcastle West which accomplished the trip at a remarkable average speed of 12.36 miles per hour! It was evident that few potential passengers had the patience of a dedicated railway enthusiast and the train, hauled by the inevitable J15, was almost empty. Tralee represents one of my lasting regrets as the Tralee and Dingle was in the midst of an almost month long hibernation which separated the monthly cattle specials from the wild west. The line was to awaken on only three or four more occasions before smoke finally vanished from the Slieve Mish mountains. My subsequent visits to Dingle by road could never recapture the atmosphere of that time, although the recreation of a portion of the old Tralee and Dingle linking the outskirts of Tralee with Blennerville offers some solace.

Following the snow and cold temperatures of County Kerry, the city of Cork provided some interesting contrasts. Named express trains were a rarity in Ireland and pride of place in the 1950s went to the 'Enterprise' which was a joint operation shared by CIÉ and the GNR(I). The crowds on the platform at Cork Glanmire Road (Kent after 1966) prior to the train's double-headed departure up Blarney bank for the first part of its journey to Dublin and Belfast injected an air of excitement and anticipation into the venerable station. At the time, the only other named trains in Ireland were the Great Northern's 'Bundoran Express', which linked Dublin to Bundoran, and CIÉ's 'Radio Train' which conveyed tourists from time to time on alternating itineraries from Dublin to Killarney or Galway.

After a visit to Cork Albert Quay station, to witness its one and only departure to all points in West Cork, and an inspection of the elderly occupants of the sidings at Rocksavage, in wet and miserable weather, it was time to move on. I chose the Saturdays only Cork–Rosslare via Dungarvan boat 'express' in 1953. The train was almost empty and I have fond memories of the generosity of the steward in the magnificent gas-lit clerestory dining car who preferred that the steaks he had prepared be eaten rather than thrown away, regardless of my ability to pay for them. This was a rare treat for the visitor from England where meat rationing still prevailed. The trip was made even more memorable by the thunderstorm which raged outside. It was altogether a most cosy and satisfying journey that night to Waterford and one, sadly, that no-one has made since March 1967.

The Waterford area provided an opportunity for visits to both a busy shed and to the isolated Tramore line. The Waterford and Tramore station at Waterford Manor was tucked away amidst a maze of back streets without benefit of much signposting to guide the traveller. It possessed its own shed and repair facilities together with an array of relics from the past including a former Clayton steam railcar set converted for use as passenger coaches. It was amazing to me that this totally isolated line of just seven miles in length had survived for so long. Perhaps it was because Tramore was the nearest seaside resort to Waterford and this was still a time when few people owned cars. My fondness for Waterford had little to do with crystal and was centred on its station, situated across the River Suir and commanding a fine view of the city. This was the junction of five rail routes and it was from here I took the branch line to New Ross and Macmine Junction. This backwater was clinging to life at the time. I remember how tantalizing it was to observe the junction with the freight only route from Muine Bheag at Palace East.

Lacking the time to travel over it at that time, I found some consolation at the delightful Macmine Junction; another peaceful retreat in the finest traditions of the Irish country junction.

Nearby Wexford, with its two stations, separated by roadside running along the quay, offered something different in the way of photographic opportunities. The same can be experienced to this day, although a new Spanish-built diesel multiple unit en route from Dublin to Rosslare may not have quite the same appeal as an Aspinall 4-4-0 and a train of vintage coaches. The former Dublin, Wicklow and Wexford route northwards to Dublin was a delightful scenic run with steam power and the prevailing speed and frequent station stops allowed plenty of time for admiring the scenery. It seemed appropriate to change at Bray and to end the journey amidst the deceptive splendour of Harcourt Street.

These memories of CIÉ relate mostly to my first visit, in 1953. Other journeys followed in the ensuing years but by then the process of modernization had gathered momentum. Since 1953, 680.84 route miles of CIÉ branch and secondary line, including 167 stations and halts, have been closed to passengers. If the services inherited by CIÉ from the Great Northern are included these totals rise to 720.34 route miles and 175 stations and halts. The carnage also affected intermediate stations on the lines that have remained in service as part of the current Iarnród Éireann (IÉ) system where a further 84 stations and halts were closed, or 89 if former GNR(I) routes are included. The magnitude of the ensuing rationalisation also reflects the impact of the abandonment of an additional 25 freight-only sections, or 32 in total when the former GNR(I) is added, for a total a total mileage of 433.50 miles. The net result is that 1153.84 CIÉ route miles have disappeared in the Irish Republic. This total does not, of course, include the rationalisation that erased the County Donegal and Londonderry & Lough Swilly from the map or sections of the GNR(I) that were never absorbed by CIÉ.

In the early 21st century there are signs that the pendulum is now beginning to swing the other way as the government applies European Community funding to the expansion of Dublin and Cork suburban services and the reinvigoration of main line services. If the pledges of politicians are translated into action, we may well be able to travel by train from Sligo to Limerick via Tuam again. Miracles have happened in Ireland and it will be interesting see how the network develops by 2010. After all, when the Listowel and Ballybunion monorail is recreated for tourists, just about anything is possible!

CÓRAS IOMPAIR ÉIREANN
RAIL NETWORK 1/1953

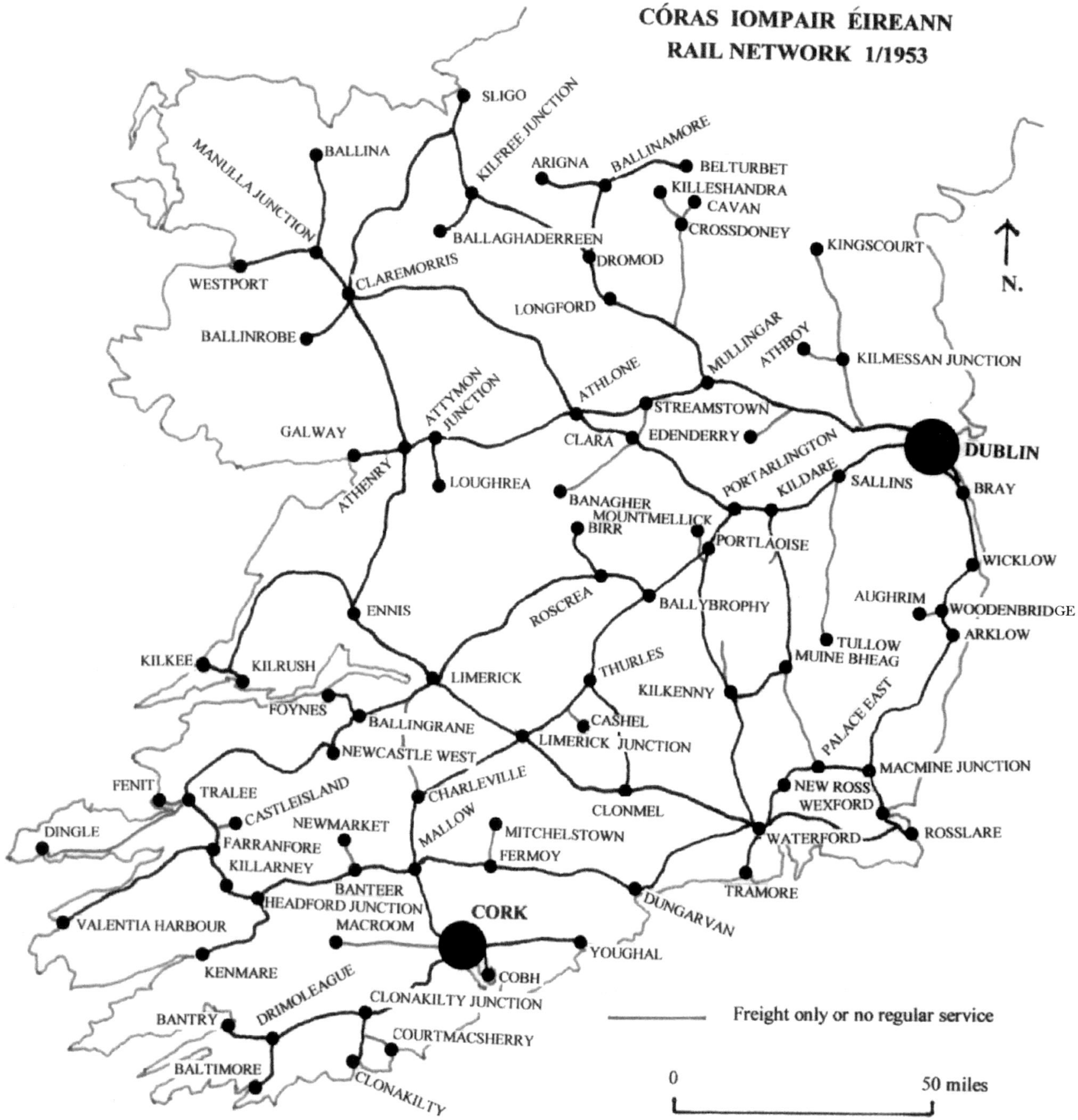

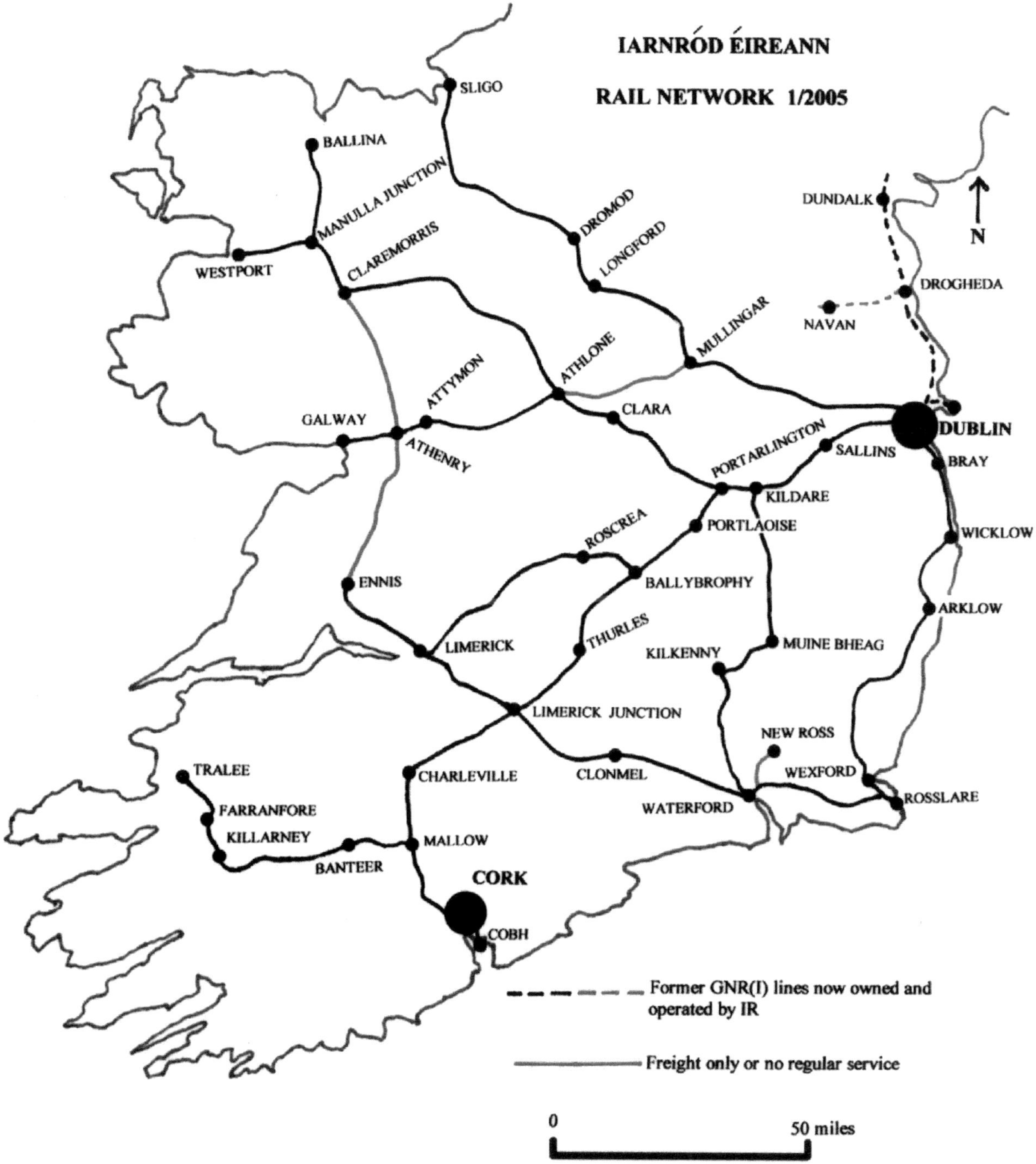

IARNRÓD ÉIREANN
RAIL NETWORK 1/2005
N
SLIGO
BALLINA
MANULLA JUNCTION
CLAREMORRIS
WESTPORT
DROMOD
LONGFORD
MULLINGAR
DUNDALK
DROGHEDA
NAVAN
ATHLONE
ATTYMON
GALWAY
ATHENRY
CLARA
DUBLIN
PORTARLINGTON
SALLINS
BRAY
KILDARE
PORTLAOISE
WICKLOW
ROSCREA
BALLYBROPHY
ENNIS
ARKLOW
LIMERICK
THURLES
KILKENNY
MUINE BHEAG
LIMERICK JUNCTION
NEW ROSS
TRALEE
CHARLEVILLE
CLONMEL
WEXFORD
FARRANFORE
WATERFORD
ROSSLARE
KILLARNEY
MALLOW
BANTEER
CORK
COBH
Former GNR(I) lines now owned and operated by IR
Freight only or no regular service
0
50 miles

Selected References:

Casserley, HC, *Outline of Irish Railway History*, David & Charles, 1974

Cronin, Kevin, *Off the Beaten Track, Irish Railway Walks*, Appletree Press, 1996

Fryer, CEJ, *The Waterford & Limerick Railway*, Oakwood Press, 2000

Murray, KA and McNeill, DB, *The Great Southern & Western Railway*, Irish Railway Record Society, 1976

Shepherd, Ernie and Beasley, Gerry, *Dublin & South Eastern Railway*, Midland Publishing Ltd, 1998

Shepherd, Ernie, *The Midland Great Western Railway of Ireland*, Midland Publishing Ltd, 1994

Johnson, Stephen, *Johnson's Atlas & Gazetteer of the Railways of Ireland*, Midland Publishing Ltd, 1997

Acknowledgements:

My thanks must go to Dr Trevor Hodge of Ottawa, Ontario, and Dr GR Siviour of Attleborough, Norfolk for kindly making available their photographs, and to Michael Bowie of Lux Photographic Services of Carleton Place, Ontario, Canada for breathing new life into my fifty year old negatives. I am also extremely grateful to Norman Johnston and Paul Savage at Colourpoint Books for turning my text and photographs into this splendid book and to Charles Friel for providing much useful additional information.

Rosslare – a port without direct road access. Class J15 No 111 propels a mainland–Rosslare Harbour Pier station shuttle service consisting of wagons conveying eight cars and a coach for passengers. Long before its transformation to a bustling Europort, the Rosslare area was a quiet corner of County Wexford, a place for restful holidays and an inconveniently designed port that appeared to be something of a white elephant.

Class D10 4-4-0 No 314, built in 1903 by Nielson Reid in Glasgow and designed by Robert Coey rounds the curve on the approach to Rosslare Harbour with the 6.50am local train from Wexford North. Beyond Ballygeary signal cabin, on the left, is the spur to Rosslare shed. To the left of the signal is Ireland's first reinforced concrete bridge, built by 'Concrete Bob' McAlpine (of the Mallaig extension and Glenfinnan fame) and opened in 1907; it was demolished about 1995.

Two J15 0-6-0s, the all-purpose workhorses of CIÉ, Nos 111 and 164 await the call of duty outside Rosslare shed. No 164 is on the left while No 111, known as 'The Sergeant' is on the right. The modern looking shed dates from 1906 and is still standing, though disconnected. The turntable is hidden by the wagons on the right. On the left is a wall constructed from sleepers and intended to keep the sand from blowing into the motion of the locomotives.

No 314 returns tender first from Rosslare Pier with the 8.15am mixed train for Wexford North; the Locomotive Inspector will not be pleased with the tender lid being left open! The absence of road access to the pier is all too obvious. To the left of No 314, down on the pier, the three steam cranes can be seen.

The Rosslare Harbour–Wexford North mixed contained some interesting contrasts in passenger rolling stock including an almost-new luggage van, a former Midland Great Western six wheeler and a former Great Southern & Western clerestory 3rd coach. The present Rosslare station is situated at this point, the single platform being to the right of the running lines.

The 7.10am all stations train to Cork via Dungarvan leaves Rosslare Harbour hauled by J15 No 164. Once again there is an eclectic mix of rolling stock.

Aspinall-designed D14 4-4-0 No 86, built in 1886, takes water at Wexford South with the 10.00am Dublin–Rosslare passenger train. The line followed an exposed waterfront route adjacent to Wexford harbour between the two stations serving the city.

The mile separating the north and south stations at Wexford is located on the quayside and necessitates low speed to protect road traffic and pedestrians. The 10.00am train from Dublin Westland Row to Rosslare negotiates this hazard at a sedate pace. Aspinall 4-4-0 No 86, one of a batch built between 1885 and 1895, is in charge.

J15 No 240, built in 1902, awaits the green flag before leaving Wexford North (now renamed Wexford O'Hanrahan and the only remaining passenger station serving Wexford) with the 7.20am from Dublin Westland Row to Rosslare Harbour train on 6 April 1953, after a loco exchange at Wexford.

The shed at Wexford North was adjacent to the station. On the occasion of my first visit, on 6 April 1953, its only occupant was, No 462, one of the two Wild 2-6-0s built in 1922 and, by the standards of the time, quite modern steam power. No 462 was a K2 built by Beyer Peacock for the Dublin and South Eastern Railway as its No 16. Along with sister No 461 it was used on heavy night goods trains between Dublin and Wexford, No 462 being Dublin-based.

D14 No 86 approaches Wexford North with the 10.00am Dublin Westland Row–Rosslare Harbour train. This part of the line is prone to flooding. Fifty-plus years on it is interesting to note that the tennis courts, to the left of the picture, are still is use.

Coey class D4 4-4-0 No 339 rounds the curve across the salt marsh into lonely Macmine Junction with the 7.20am Dublin Westland Row–Rosslare Harbour train. The junction with the line to Waterford via New Ross is visible in the centre background. No 339 was built in 1908 for use on Mallow to Rosslare express services.

The quiet country station at Killinick was a comparative rarity in Ireland having, In common with other intermediate stations between Rosslare Strand and Waterford, an island platform. Serving a thinly-populated rural area it handled one passenger train in each direction on weekdays with an extra on Saturdays. Along with Duncormick on the same line it was closed in 1976. Local services in southeast Wexford in the 1950s could best be described as vestigial.

Aspinall's D17 class 4-4-0s were built between 1883 and 1890. It was fitting that among these veterans No 14, dating from 1888, was engaged on light duties such as the morning Waterford–Macmine Junction service, seen here at New Ross.

In the mid 1950s Bray was on the threshold of dieselization. On a wet and dreary 11 September 1957, I3 class 0-6-2T No 673, a Harty design dating from 1933, prepares to leave with a suburban service for Dublin Amiens Street. The third coach is a Park Royal.

A brand new 550hp diesel electric built by Metropolitan Vickers No C227 shunts a motley array of rolling stock at Bray as part of its running-in process. These underpowered units were designed for branch line duties and would not have been ideal for Dublin suburban work. The initial aluminium/silver livery applied to CIÉ's first generation diesels was not compatible with the Irish climate and rapidly projected a very tarnished image.

The AEC diesel railcars had been regular performers on the Greystones–Bray–Dublin Harcourt Street service since the mid 1950s. The commodious station at Bray was well designed for its ongoing evolution from seaside resort destination to rapid transit hub for Dublin commuters. The AEC Park Royal railcars were built between 1952 and 1954 and were withdrawn between 1972 and 1987; three damaged vehicles were converted to powered intermediates.

Waterford's station, now Waterford Plunkett, offers the traveller an intriguing vista of the city on the opposite bank of the river Suir. In the early 1950s the station and its nearby loco shed revealed an equally intriguing prospect of steam traction serving two routes to Dublin and four other cross country lines to Mallow, Limerick Junction, Rosslare and Macmine Junction. All were characterized by infrequent services, vintage steam power and rolling stock. Stately D17 No 14 awaits departure with the 9.05am for Macmine Junction, a 33 mile journey to be accomplished in a sedate 73 minutes. This is Platform 2 and it, along with Platform 1, are now a car park at the east end of the station.

There was plenty of activity at the former Waterford, Limerick and Western shed at Waterford. Locomotives present included a Coey class D10 4-4-0 No 314 of 1903 vintage, class J13 'Jumbo', J15 0-6-0 No 116, built at Inchicore in 1896 and a Maunsell Mogul, which looks to be of the K1 class, whose number was unfortunately not recorded. Note the open back to the cab on 'Jumbo', a feature rarely seen in photographs.

My bias at the time was firmly in favour of the class D17 4-4-0s which seemed to embody what a proper steam locomotive should really look like. Here, on 5 April 1953, No 3 shares a siding outside Waterford shed with J15 No 153 and a row of other delightful antiques. No 3 was built in 1890 and lasted until 1957. The loco on the left is a J4 class 0-6-0 while that on the right is No 153, built by Beyer Peacock in 1868 and scrapped in 1954.

The unique 0-6-0T *Jumbo*, inexplicably lacking a number, was a rebuild of a McDonnell 0-6-4T banking engine built in 1876. It was a feature of Waterford from the early 1900s and was still busy as shed pilot in the early 1950s. It was hauled away for scrap in 1957.

Across the city, and not far from the Waterford Glass factory, was a real curiosity – the 7½ mile long and totally isolated Waterford & Tramore line. Waterford Manor station, minus its trainshed roof, radiated a distinctly forlorn atmosphere but all the essentials remained including a carriage shed (right foreground), loco shed and shops (right background) and water tower (on the platform).

Turntable limitations at Waterford Manor effectively restricted locomotive types that could be employed and thereby added to the charm of the line. The author erroneously reported that Atock J26 0-6-0T No 552 was in the process of being scrapped and was taken firmly to task by contributors to the *Railway Observer*. It was in fact awaiting a boiler, which was probably being overhauled at Inchicore. The custom on the Waterford and Tramore was to have one engine in steam, one spare and the third reduced temporarily to a mass of spare parts scattered around the very cramped premises at Waterford Manor.

Three two-car articulated sets, built originally as Clayton steam railcars in 1928, were transferred to the Tramore line in 1933 where their greater passenger capacity made them the preferred rolling stock for summer peak traffic and on race days. They soldiered on until dieselisation in November 1954.

Class J26 No 553, built as MGWR No 108 *Swallow* in 1891 by Kitson's, is approaching Tramore with a train from Waterford. It was scrapped in 1955 and its boiler exported to Spain. The lower quadrant signal, one of only two on the line, protected the coastal terminus. Both signal and points were manually operated by the head porter at Tramore who walked, or sometimes ran, from the station to perform the task. *Dr Trevor Hodge*

No 553 is ready for a return trip to Waterford from Tramore. The trainshed survived there until the closure of the line in January 1961. The J26 class locos working on the Tramore line received several modifications including an extension of the cab, to totally enclose the coal bunker and rebuilt leading and cab steps. *Dr Trevor Hodge*

A long lost boat train, the 6.15am Saturdays only Rosslare Harbour–Cork via Dungarvan buffet car train, pauses at Mallow for passengers connecting to the Killarney and Tralee line. A remarkably clean class D11 4-4-0 No 302, a Coey design of 1900, provides the power for this 135 mile, 4 hours 15 minute cross country journey. No 302 was once named *Lord Roberts*. It was cut up at Waterford some time after 1957.

In the heyday of the Irish railway network there were a significant number of isolated country junctions serving little or no local population. In the early 1950s eight such interchange points (Attymon Junction, Clonakilty Junction, Headford Junction, Kilfree Junction, Limerick Junction, Macmine Junction, Manulla Junction and Moyasta Junction) were open on CIÉ; in 2005 only three remained open. A good example was Headford Junction on the Mallow–Tralee line, seen here in August 1957, where passengers changed for the scenic and long lamented Kenmare branch. Class J15 0-6-0 No 156, one of a series built to the design of McDonnell between 1866 and 1903 was typical power on this branch hauling a characteristically eclectic variety of elderly rolling stock. Trains ceased running to Kenmare in 1960 and Headford Junction has faded from memory since its demise in 1963, its site being unnoticed from trains en route to Killarney and Tralee.

Dr Gerald Siviour

It doesn't snow very often at Easter in Tralee but it did on Easter Sunday in April 1953 when I visited Tralee shed. My visit revealed an array of J11s and J15s, the J15 on the extreme left being a Coey example. In the background is the steam crane used for coaling locos. The trainshed roof is visible beyond that and, to its right, the distinctive warehouse in Ashe Street where the Tralee & Dingle connecting line to the goods yard ran along the street.

A particularly frustrating experience was to visit the slumbering Tralee & Dingle line at the wrong time of the month for the monthly cattle train to Dingle. Kerr Stuart KN2 2-6-0Ts Nos 1T and 3T, in semi-retirement, await the next challenging assault on the mountains.

Passengers had long deserted the Tralee & Dingle station in Tralee and the cattle wagons were decaying gently in this funereal scene, taken on 3 April 1953. Note the gate at the far end through which the engines ran to get coal in the broad gauge goods yard. The warehouse, which belonged to R McCowen and Sons and mentioned on page 39, dominates the skyline; it is still there. The station building survives in fine order, in use as offices.

An unpleasantly wet and chilly walk along the narrow gauge revealed that the first station, Tralee Basin, had become a dwelling with, of course, the inevitable chickens. The level crossing gates are on the Blennerville road and the Tralee terminus of the present preserved line is on the left, not far beyond.

Cloud cover on the Slieve Mish mountains towards Castlegregory Junction did not encourage any further exploration beyond the derelict station at Blennerville. The present line's platform is on the trackbed shown here and the line, with its loop, is on the site of the building.

The North Kerry line had the air of a forgotten backwater and the solitary weekdays-only train from Limerick to Tralee was both slower and less frequent than the parallel CIÉ bus service. Newcastle West station had a track layout that reflected the historical evolution of the line. A highlight of its day was the crossing of the Limerick–Tralee passenger and the Tralee–Limerick freight hauled, on 2 April 1953, by 1902-built Coey J15 No 241. Milk and cream cans were becoming increasingly rare on CIÉ at the time but there was still evidence of livestock traffic. A turntable and watering facilities betrayed the historical significance of Newcastle West as a railhead.

J15 No 107, built at Inchicore in 1881, waits at Newcastle West for 17 minutes to pass the Limerick bound freight before resuming its leisurely all stations journey to Tralee. The 43¼ miles separating Limerick and Tralee were covered in 205 minutes giving some credibility to the CIÉ logo at that date. For a visiting enthusiast it was an experience akin to sipping a fine wine. No 107 was withdrawn in 1957 and exported to Spain, for scrapping, in 1958.

Newcastle West was a dead end, where all trains had to reverse. The trainshed and stop blocks were a reminder that the station was a terminus between 1867 and 1880 before the line was extended westwards to Tralee; there were actually two terminal stations, side by side. The Rathkeale and Newcastle Junction Railway opened to here on 1 January 1867 while the Limerick and Kerry Railway did not arrive from the Tralee direction until a few days before Christmas 1980.

The departure of the 'Enterprise' express to Dublin and Belfast was always a big occasion at Cork Glanmire Road (now Cork Kent). Shortly after 1pm on 4 April 1953, Class B2a 4-6-0 No 406, immaculately turned out in CIÉ green livery, with its train of equally spotless GNR(I) coaches was, as the saying goes, a sight for tired eyes. No 406 was built at Inchicore in 1921 and here has the Caprotti valve gear fitted in 1930.

A contrast in colour and styles. Class D17 No 20 is ready to perform pilot duties for No 406 and the 'Enterprise' express through the smoke laden tunnel and up the bank to Rathpeacon. By the time this photograph was taken No 20 was 63 years old, having been constructed at Inchicore in 1890.

The only other terminus remaining open in Cork in the early 1950s was Cork Albert Quay. This gateway to the straggling Cork, Bandon and South Coast network offered quite a contrast to hustle and bustle of Glanmire Road with but one departure scheduled on weekdays only. Notwithstanding the paucity of trains it boasted a bookstall and even sold platform tickets to the casual visitor.

The high point of the day at Cork Albert Quay was the departure of the 5.40pm train for all stations to Bantry. More accurately this service could be described as the 5.40pm to everywhere in southwest Cork since it had rail connections for Clonakilty, Skibbereen and Baltimore and bus linkages to far off Schull and Goleen. This all-purpose train was in the capable hands of Beyer Peacock 4-6-0T No 463 which would work through to Bantry. No 463 was built as Cork, Bandon and South Coast Railway No 4 in 1919.

The Cork Albert Quay platform ticket was good value for twopence and gave access to the delights of the adjoining 'shed'. (The place is usually referred to as Rocksavage.) In reality it was a cramped site where a bridge provided meagre shelter to a veritable locomotive museum whose bedraggled components were huddled together like desperate vagrants. A quick examination of the inmates certainly cast strong doubts as whether some would ever steam again. In spite of the atrocious weather it was an unforgettable experience. No 37 (left) was a C7 class built in 1894. Beyond is No 552, a J26 class built by Kitsons in 1894 as MGWR No 117 *Moy*.

We now move up the main line to Dublin and call at Portarlington where we see the beginnings of the transition that was taking place on CIÉ. AEC railcars Nos 2616/7 with vintage trailer and van form the 8.10am Waterford–Dublin Kingsbridge via Portlaoise. It's 2 April 1953 and No 2617 is in pristine condition, being just a matter of days old. It was burned in June 1957, rebuilt in in 1960 and converted to a powered intermediate in 1961. Withdrawal came in 1985.

Notwithstanding the advent of dieselisation on certain main lines, time stood still elsewhere. No 587, built by Sharp Stewart in 1895 as MGWR LM class No 133 *Titan*, has been turned and shunted into the siding alongside the down main line at Portarlington after working the 8.40am from Athlone. At that time this route was a quiet backwater through the bogs of Counties Offaly and Westmeath with two weekdays-only passenger services in each direction. Few would then have predicted its later elevation to main line status.

The former Midland Great Western Railway station at Athlone was the principal and only station served by passenger trains in the 1950s. J18 No 587 is about to depart with the 8.40am to Portarlington via Tullamore. Dublin to Galway and Westport trains then ran via Mullingar and the former Great Southern and Western station in Athlone had remained closed to passengers since 1925. The situation was reversed in 1985 with the diversion of Galway and Mayo services to the Tullamore route and the closure of the MGWR station. Interestingly the possibility of reactivating the Athlone to Mullingar via Moate route could see a further revival of fortunes for this station. Note the GNR(I) van in the bay platform.

A D10 4-4-0 gets into its stride on the curve out of Ballybrophy with the 10.00am Dublin Kingsbridge to Limerick via Roscrea train. It would be most unusual to see trains of this length on this line today.

Class D17 No 59 pauses at Athenry during its stately progress on the 11.55am Galway to Tuam service. This was as delightful a Victorian ensemble as one could wish to discover during the last days of steam on CIÉ. Passengers on the down platform await the arrival of the 8.40am Dublin Westland Row to Galway mail train. No 59 had featured in the film *The Quiet Man*, part of which was shot at Ballyglunin, although the film makers called the station Castletown. There remains a glimmer of hope that one may once again be able to reach Tuam by passenger train.

Another dignified Aspinall product, D14 4-4-0 No 89, makes a nine minute stop at Claremorris with the 8.45am Sligo–Limerick train to make the connection with the 10.00am from Westport to Dublin Westland Row and the 10.10am from Ballinrobe. No 89 was built at Inchicore in 1886 as a class D13 but was reclassified D14 in 1933 when she was given a superheated boiler. At the same time she received a larger cab, apparently for working the 3.30am Dublin to Cork newspaper train. Claremorris may yet witness the revival of the 'Burma Road' – the west is awake!

The 9.25am Dublin Westland Row to Sligo on 30 March 1953, hauled by Cusack D5 4-4-0 No 550, was my first footplate experience on CIÉ. It was made all the more memorable by my disastrous attempts to maintain adequate boiler pressure with poor coal and powdery briquettes. All this amused the crew and made little impression on the passengers who accepted late running and a countryside obscured by clouds of smoke as the norms. Everyone was glad of this break at Longford – not least Driver John Byrne who was carefully nursing his steed along with some hopes of eventually reaching Sligo, still two hours away. No 550 was built at the Broadstone in 1905 as MGWR No 125, the only A1 class loco built.

It was with some relief that I left No 550 at Dromod. This photograph is a tribute to Driver John Byrne and his mate, Fireman Joe Ledwith, from Broadstone shed and all of their colleagues who strove so manfully to keep the trains running during the dying gasps of steam operation. The station building for the Cavan & Letrim section can just be glimpsed to the extreme left of the picture.

First generation diesel electric power on CIÉ was not notably successful. With its silver livery falling victim to grime, No A5 built by Metropolitan-Vickers/Crossley in 1955, pulls away from Dromod with the morning Dublin–Sligo train on 28 August 1957. The cross platform freight interchange with the Cavan and Leitrim section is visible on the left. Now the second generation General Motors diesel power is about to be supplanted by new multiple units from Europe – tempus fugit!

There's more to this engine than meets the eye. Despite carrying the number 409 this is actually class B2 No 404, built by Armstrong Whitworth in 1923. When the No 404 was condemned in 1930 someone swopped her plates with the 'real' No 409 and the latter was scrapped. The new No 409 was converted to two cylinders in 1935 and became class B2a. It is seen at Inchicore on 29 March 1953.

Dieselisation increased the flow of withdrawn steam locomotives arriving at Inchicore for breaking up. The process was unhurried and many condemned locomotives lingered there for long periods. Ex Cork, Blackrock & Passage and Cavan & Leitrim class FNI 2-4-2T No 13, ex West Clare 4-6-0T No 11c and J15 0-6-0 No 229 await their fate. No 13 was built as CB&P No 7 in 1899, No 11c was built in 1899 (and was once named *Kilkee)* and No 229 was built at Inchicore in 1903.

Bulleid's first experimental turf burner, rebuilt from class K3 2-6-0 No 356, was tucked away in a corner at Inchicore (in disgrace!). No 356 began life as one of a class of seven 0-6-0s built by North British in 1903. She was regarded as one of the best of the class and reportedly did a spell on the Dublin to Cork night mail train. This is No 356 in her first rebuilt form – the preheaters alongside the boiler barrel were later changed to an upright oval shape. In retrospect the security concerns relating to this locomotive do not seem to have been altogether justified.

11 September 1957 and Metropolitan-Vickers/Crossley A41 passes Amiens Street with a Dublin Westland Row to Galway train composed of the usual mix of rolling stock and typifying a period of major and continuing change on CIÉ. The signal cabin controlled the GSR/CIÉ side of the station. It closed when the Dublin Area Rapid Transit system (DART) came into being in April 1984. The colour light signals dated from 1936.